DIVISIONAL AND OTHER SIGNS

DIVISIONAL AND OTHER SIGNS

COLLECTED AND ILLUSTRATED BY

V. WHEELER-HOLOHAN

Captain, 12th London Regiment

LONDON :
JOHN MURRAY, ALBEMARLE STREET, W.
1920

First published in 1920 by
John Murray, Albemarle Street, London.

CONTENTS

CONTENTS

CONTENTS

CONTENTS

PREFACE

THE origin of the Army, Corps and Divisional Sign was the necessity of having some means of immediately recognising the transport and personnel of any unit or formation. It was also intended to mystify the enemy, and to prevent his discovering the identity of the Corps or Division which was opposing him at any particular portion of the Front. In the early days of the War, transport vehicles, headquarter boards, staff armlets and so on all bore the number of the Corps or Division, plain for friend or foe alike to see. The coming of the sign or badge changed that.

After a time, however, the sign commenced to have a greater meaning. The esprit de corps of the New Army Divisions was derived, to a great extent, from their Territorial designation. North countrymen emulated the deeds of men from London and from the West, all fired with pride of the Northern Counties, of the Capital, of the West.

But casualties were enormous, and it
was often impossible to fill the gaps with
the reserves intended for particular units.
Gradually men became mixed. An Irish
Division might be found to be composed
largely of soldiers from all parts of the four
Kingdoms—a London Division would number a goodly portion of men from any part
of England but London. The old, original
esprit de corps—*but not the morale*—gradually faded away. Then a rather astonishing
thing happened ; the Divisional Sign
brought out a new feeling of esprit de corps
throughout our Armies. Officers and men
began to notice other signs and to take an
interest in them. The badge became to
them a visible mark which distinguished
them, and they became intensely proud
of their own sign.

Speaking generally, there would appear
to be five types of sign or badge. There
was, first of all, the design which was purely
a distinguishing mark and had no history
or particular origin—easy to draw and easy
to recognise. Then there was what might
be called the " Territorial " type, such as
the Welsh Dragon of the 38th Division, the
Thistle of the 9th (Scottish) Division, the
Red Rose of the 55th (West Lancashire)

Division. Again, there was the cypher
type, possibly the most interesting of them
all—the three sevens of the 21st, the LXI
of the 61st, the ATN of the 18th, to mention
a few of them, some of them examples of
great cleverness and ingenuity. The fourth
type was the " rebus," or pun upon the
names of the General Officers commanding
—to take two examples, the M and AXES
of Maxse's Eighteenth Corps, the Bear and
Iceberg of Snow's Seventh Corps. Lastly,
there is the " Battle Honour " type,
exemplified by the Acorn on the Sign of
the 40th, or the Umbrella of the 54th
Divisions.

In every case the diagrams which follow
were drawn from actual badges and signs.
Nearly all the histories and origins were
obtained from the General Officers who
commanded the various Corps and Divisions,
and I cannot express sufficiently the debt
I owe to them for the patience and kindness
with which they corrected my rough
sketches and supplied me with information.
My thanks are due also to the publisher—
Lieutenant-Colonel John Murray, D.S.O.
It is not hard to write a book, but it is very
hard to get it published. I was fortunate
in encountering a soldier who had taken a

great interest in these signs, and he has enabled me to bring out this little work.

In conclusion, I am only too ready to admit that the book falls far short of what I would have liked it to be. Black and white diagrams have been used for two reasons. Firstly, to enable the publication to be brought out at a low price; and, secondly, because some formations used the sign in various colours, and therefore no one colour is specially correct. But, such as the result is, I would be very glad to think that it may afford a few minutes' interest to some of those who served together in the Great War, to the ultimate detriment of the Hun.

V. WHEELER-HOLOHAN.

London,
  February, 1920.

GENERAL H.Q., B.E.F. FRANCE

The G.H.Q. Sign and Armlet had no
history. The top half was red, the bottom
half blue. It was formed in 1914.

FIRST ARMY

The First Army G.H.Q. cars, transport, etc., were distinguished by a narrow white line, which was painted on the back of each vehicle. The above sketch was drawn from one of the actual G.H.Q. cars, and the sign of the white line—apart from its simplicity —would seem to have no particular history.

SECOND ARMY

The Second Army never had a special sign. The Army lorries, etc., bore the red and black Army colours with " II " inscribed thereon. The Staff Armlets bore no sign or mark. In the diagram above the shaded portion shows the red part.

THIRD ARMY

The Third Army sign was a bull's eye in
black on a white circular ground. This
was placed upon the usual army brassard,
a black bar between two red bars. In the
above diagram the red portion is shaded.
The top and bottom of the sign were edged
with a narrow line of yellow. It came into
use about June 1917, just after Sir Julian
Byng had succeeded Sir Edmund Allenby
as Commander. The centre of the design
was built up from the "sobriquets" of these
two eminent soldiers.

FOURTH ARMY

The Boar's Head of the Fourth Army was, perhaps, one of the best known signs in France.

The history of the sign has relation to a visit paid by the G.O.C.—Lord Rawlinson (or Sir Henry Rawlinson, as he then was) to a forest owned by the Duke of Westminster in the South of France, where the sport of boar hunting was indulged in.

In the Spring of 1917, shortly after his return, the question of an Army sign was brought to his attention, and he selected the Boar's Head in memory of the sport he had enjoyed during his brief leave.

FIFTH ARMY

The badge of the Fifth Army (commanded at the time the sign was instituted by General Sir Hubert Gough, K.C.B., K.C.V.O.) was a racing fox in red, with a white tip to his brush.

It has no particular history, and was adopted during the Battle of the Somme.

THE CAVALRY CORPS

The Cavalry Corps sign was originally a female head, but was altered subsequently to "St. George and the Dragon," the patron saint of the Cavalry Soldier.

It was painted on a circular plate about ten inches in diameter, and was copied from the figures on the British £1 note. The horse was white and St. George wore a red cloak ; the dragon was green with a red tongue and eyes, and the protruding end of the lance was also red.

I. CORPS

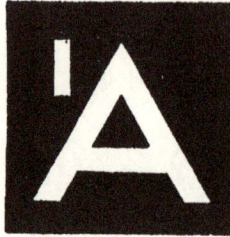

The above sign speaks for itself. It was generally painted with white lettering on a dark background. Many officers and men used to think that the sign was that of the First Army, but it soon dawned upon some of them that if it was the First Army sign it was much too obvious.

II. CORPS

This was the famous Corps commanded by Lieut.-General Sir Charles Fergusson and, after May, 1916, by Lieut.-General Sir Claude Jacob. The sign was the usual red and white corps badge—two red bars with a white bar in the middle—but the latter was charged with a red six-pointed star. In the diagram above, the black part represents the red portion of the sign.

III. CORPS

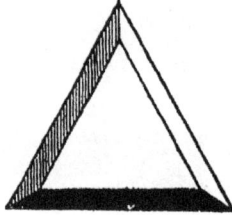

The III. Corps sign was an equilateral triangle, the base being black, the left side red, and the third side white. This sign was devised by Lieut.-General Sir William Pulteney, K.C.B., K.C.M.G., D.S.O., red, black and white being his racing colours. When Lieut.-General Sir Richard Butler K.C.M.G., C.B., succeeded him in the command of the Corps, the same sign was retained.

IV. CORPS

This Corps was distinguished by the usual Corps colours, two red bars with a white one between them, the latter charged with an oblong black patch. In the diagram above the shaded part represents the red portion.

The explanation is simple. The sign was originally composed of the ordinary Corps colours—red and white—with the number of the Corps in the centre of the white strip. When the order appeared which prohibited the use of any sign which might disclose the number or name of any formation, the black patch was used to cover the number and eventually became part of the IV. Corps device.

V. CORPS

This was the famous Corps commanded in turn by Field-Marshal Lord Allenby, General Plumer, and Lieut.-General Sir Edward Fanshawe. It's sign does not appear to have any history apart from the five points for " FIVE."

VI. CORPS

This was one of the best known signs in the B.E.F. The Corps known occasionally as the " Bulldog " Corps, a title it would appear to have earned during the heavy fighting in 1917 and 1918, when it was commanded by Lieut.-General Sir Aylmer Haldane, K.C.B., D.S.O.

VII. CORPS

This Corps was commanded for a long
time by Lieut.-General Sir T. D'O. Snow,
K.C.B.—in fact, it was really identified
with him. The sign was a white polar bear
—a " snowy " bear, with Ursa Major also
in the design, it's seven stars indicating the
Seventh Corps. The position of the stars
of the constellation as shewn above are not
correct, but the sketch is a faithful copy of
one of the actual signs.

VIII. CORPS

"The Horn of the Hunter."

This Corps was formed on Gallipoli Peninsula in May, 1915, and was commanded from that date till after the cessation of hostilities by Lieut.-General Sir Aylmer Hunter-Weston, K.C.B., D.S.O., M.P.

The Corps sign was his heraldic bearing : "A hunting horn vert (green) stringed and garnished gules (red)." The Hunters of Hunterston hold their land under a charter dating from 1200 as prefects of the Royal Hunters in the West of Scotland, and as such were given the horn of the hunter for their arms.

IX. CORPS

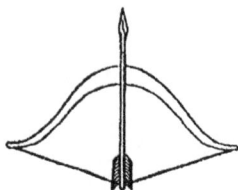

The original IX. Corps which served in Gallipoli was broken up after the evacuation. When the new Corps was formed in June, 1916, Lieut.-General Sir Alexander Hamilton Gordon, K.C.B., who was appointed to command it, utilised a portion of his crest, and this badge was carried on by his successor, Lieut.-General Sir Walter Braithwaite, K.C.B.

X CORPS

The Tenth Corps' sign was the ordinary Corps badge of two red bars with a white one in the middle. When the Corps was first formed in July, 1915, the Corps badge with X on it was used ; but when orders came through that no more numbers were to be shewn, the X was removed ; and as various signs were hastily adopted by the other Army Corps, the Tenth simply kept the original Corps colours.

XI. CORPS

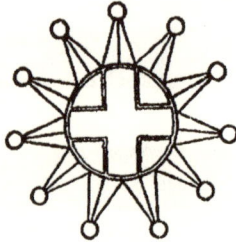

This Corps' sign was a gold star of eleven points (the number of the Corps), each point topped with a gold ball. The disc in the centre was red, and on it was a white cross. The top ray of the star, it will be noticed, exactly coincided with the top bar of the cross. The device in the middle was taken from the distinguishing flag of a Corps Headquarters—a white cross on a red ground.

XIII. CORPS

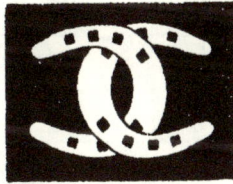

The ground of this sign was black, the horseshoe with its points to the left was red, and the other white. It was designed in November, 1915, by Colonel Glyn, Camp Commandant of the XIII. Corps, and represents " C.C. " for " Congreve's Corps and Good Luck," Lieut.-General Sir Walter Congreve, V.C., K.C.B., M.V.O., being at the time the sign was adopted the Corps Commander.

XIV. CORPS

This Corps' sign was very distinctive—
a chequer of sixteen squares of blue and
white. In the diagram above the blue
portion is represented by shading. The
sign has no particular history.

XV. CORPS

The XV. Corps' sign was never very clearly defined. For a time, the circular device shown above on the right was in use. Its colours were red and white (the black part representing red).

The " Y " sign was in fairly general use, and was really the Corps sign. The author has been given two reasons as to its origin.

The first, which is generally accepted as the correct one, is that the letter " Y "—by a stretch of imagination—may be said to represent three Roman V's for XV.

The second, is that when the order for the Corps to be formed was received in Egypt, it was given the title " Y " Corps, presumably because the number had not yet been decided upon.

Just before the Armistice, a new Corps sign was designed, but it was never adopted.

XVI. CORPS

This Corps was commanded for over three years by Lieut.-General Sir Charles Briggs, K.C.B., K.C.M.G. During the whole of this time the Corps never had any distinctive sign, and never flew even the usual flag.

XVII. CORPS

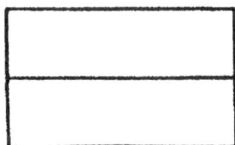

This Corps' sign was an oblong divided into two bands, the top one being green and the other white. As far as the author is aware, it had no particular history or meaning. The general opinion of several officers who have been consulted is that it was intended to be just a " distinguishing mark which should be as simple as possible."

XVIII. CORPS

This Corps was in existence from January 15th, 1917, to June 25th, 1918. During the whole of that time it had only one Commander—Lieut.-General Sir Ivor Maxse, K.C.B., C.V.O., D.S.O. Its sign was well known in France, being two crossed battle axes and the initial M, signifying M AXES, or Maxse's Corps.

XIX. CORPS

This Corps' sign, like that of the XVIII.,
was simply a pun on the name of its G.O.C
—Lieut.-General Sir Herbert Watts, K.C.B.
C.M.G. Three interrogation marks or
" Whats " in white on a red background.

XX. CORPS

The XX. Corps never really had a sign,
and the one shown above—of which the
author does not know the history—came
out very late in the War, about March, 1918.

XXI. CORPS

The XXI. Corps, commanded in Palestine by Lieut.-General Sir Edward Bulfin, K.C.B., C.V.O., utilised as its sign the green four-leaved shamrock—perhaps a concession to the nationality of its G.O.C. On each of the top and side leaves appeared the Roman figure VII—three sevens for twenty-one—and on the lower leaf the word "Corps."

Many direction boards bearing this sign are still to be seen standing in parts of Palestine—a telling testimony of the marches and battles in which the XXI. Corps participated.

XXII. CORPS

This Corps, commanded by Lieut.-General
Sir A. J. Godley, K.C.B., K.C.M.G., was
known by its foxhound. The actual sign
was designed and drawn by Colonel Magnus.
The origin was simple—there were two
Masters of Foxhounds on the Corps Staff.
The sign was also regarded as a grim allusion to the eventual hunt of the enemy
which was bound to come in time.

THE AUSTRALIAN CORPS

The Australian Corps' H.Q. sign was a hollow triangle. It appears to have no particular history or origin. Several officers and men have told the author that it was intended to use the letter " A." This would have been too obvious, so the projecting legs of the initial were removed, leaving the hollow triangle shown above.

(See also Australian Divisions.)

The golden initial " A," often seen on the Corps and Divisional Signs, signified that the wearer had taken part in the Gallipoli Campaign.

1st CAVALRY DIVISION

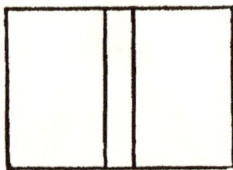

The 1st Cavalry Division had as their sign a white oblong with a red stripe in its centre. This sign—as far as the author can ascertain—has no particular history.

2ND CAVALRY DIVISION

This sign, like that of the 3rd Cavalry Division has no particular history. The horseshoes have toeclips and nine holes each. The left-hand one was painted in white, and the other, which overlaps it, in red.

Originally the two horseshoes were shown pointing downwards, but in 1916 they were reversed by Lieut.-General Sir Philip Chetwode, Bt., K.C.M.G., C.B., D.S.O., on the grounds that " If a horseshoe is hung upside down the luck is said to run out at the bottom ! "

3RD CAVALRY DIVISION

There is no particular history attached
to the origin of this sign. When all the
Divisions were ordered to adopt signs, the
Divisional Commander thought the horseshoe would be appropriate, and decided
to repeat the number of the Division by the
number of the shoes.

These three latter have no front clips, and
contain only five holes each. They were
painted in white on the wagons, etc.

THE GUARDS DIVISION

Possibly the best known Divisional sign in the British Expeditionary Force was the " eye " of the Guards. This was the mark borne on the transport, and is illustrated above. The designer, the late Major Sir Eric Avery, Bart., M.C. (who commanded the Divisional M.T. Company) was told to design something " plain, clear and unforgettable." The now famous " eye " was the result.

The pupil was in black, the rest of the eye in white, all on a blue background, while there was a red edging to the shield. A narrow rim of gold bordered the red edging on each side.

Attached troops—R.E., R.A.M.C., etc.—wore a " G " on small cloth shields of different colours according to the units. Officers had it worked in gold thread, other ranks simply a brass initial.

1st DIVISION

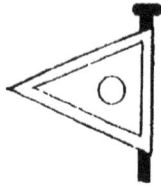

The sign of the First Division was a blue triangular flag, with a white edge. The centre was charged with a white spot, and the flagstaff was painted in black.

This flag (Marine Signals) represents the word " One "—hence its application to this Division.

2ND DIVISION

The Second Division was marked by
three eight-pointed stars on a black oval
ground. The centre star was red, the others
white. The two white stars were said to
represent the Second Division, the red star
the First Corps, or " The Second Division
of the First Corps."

3RD DIVISION

This was one of the simplest Divisional signs, and amply fulfilled its purpose as a secret sign which would not divulge the number of the Division to unauthorised persons. The G.O.C.—Lieut.-General Sir Aylmer Haldane, K.C.B., D.S.O., devised a simple mark which could be drawn rapidly by any unskilled draughtsman, say for example, when chalking up the sign on the walls of billets, etc. The cross was one of the charges in his Armorial Bearings.

The badge was simply a circle with a cross, in yellow. It was never clearly defined whether the cross lines went over or under the circle. The diagram shows the yellow cloth mark as it was worn on the sleeves by personnel.

4TH DIVISION

The Fourth Division was commanded at
the time signs were instituted by Major-
General the Hon. Sir William Lambton,
K.C.B., C.M.G., D.S.O. He adopted the
crest of the Lambton family—" A Ram's
Head "—as the Divisional sign.

It was cut out of cloth of various colours
and worn on the shoulders by the personnel, and stencilled in various colours on
the wagons. A peculiar feature in some of
the latter signs was the omission of the
ram's eyes.

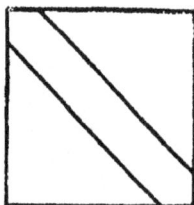

When the order came that a sign was to be adopted, a yellow diagonal bar was utilised, which was placed across the various official unit marks. As time went on, however, a blue square was substituted for the latter, and at the end of the war the sign of the Division was generally recognised as being a blue square with a yellow diagonal bar.

6TH DIVISION

This sign was simply a white circle or ring on a black square. It would appear that there is no particular history attached to it.

7TH DIVISION

This Division was known by the white disc on a black ground. The author, although in communication with many officers of this Division, has been unable to ascertain if there is any history attached to its origin. The general consensus of opinion is that it has no history.

8TH DIVISION

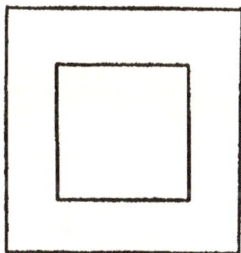

No particular history attaches to the sign
of the 8th Division—" A red square within
a white one." It was a very simple mark,
and very easily recognised.

9TH (SCOTTISH) DIVISION

The sign of the 9th (Scottish) Division needs no explanation. It was worn by all ranks on each arm below the shoulder, the thistle being made of silver or white metal mounted on a circular piece of dark blue cloth.

10TH (IRISH) DIVISION

This was the 10th Division—commanded by Lieut.-General Sir Bryan Mahon, K.C.V.O., C.B., D.S.O., which served in Gallipoli, and afterwards in Egypt.

When in December, 1915, Major-General J. R. Longley, C.B., took over command, he obtained permission for all ranks to wear a narrow green stripe on the shoulder strap.

Later on, when Headquarters asked for suggestions for a Divisional sign, a green shamrock was proposed, but this was the mark of another Irish Division—the 16th. Accordingly, a narrow green strip, about 10″ long by 3″ in width was adopted.

11TH (NORTHERN) DIVISION

This Divisional Sign was the subject of much curiosity as to its origin, and comparatively few officers and men—even in the Division itself—knew anything about it. The Division was in Egypt at the time the order was received for it to select a Divisional Badge, and the Sign which is illustrated above was chosen. It was supposed to represent the "Ankus" or the "Key of Life," but to make it more easily seen the base was made wider than in the original cross.

12TH (EASTERN) DIVISION

The ace of spades of the 12th Division is another sign which seems to have no particular origin. It was often seen charged with the regimental crests of various units in the Division.

13TH (WESTERN) DIVISION

The 13th Division was known by its black horseshoe "points upwards." It was chosen for the sake of luck, with possible reference to the fact that some of the home papers at one time christened it the " Iron Division," and the men rather fancied this title.

14TH (LIGHT) DIVISION

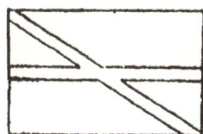

This was a remarkable sign. The colour of the oblong—green—represented the light Division. Many people were under the impression that the two white lines thereon were taken from the diagram of the Fourteenth Proposition of Euclid, but two crossed lines are, however, that of the Fifteenth Proposition!

15TH (SCOTTISH) DIVISION

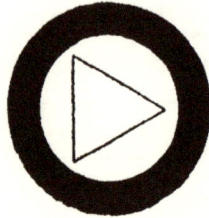

This is another sign which possesses no particular history. It was simply a red Brigade-Commander's flag on a white background, surrounded by a black circle.

16TH (IRISH) DIVISION
" Everywhere and always Faithful."

This Division had two signs. The monogram " L P " was painted on the transport wagons, Headquarter boards, etc. It was adopted by the G.O.C., Major-General Sir William Hickie, K.C.B., out of compliment to Lieut.-General Sir Lawrence Parsons, K.C.B., who raised the Division and was its first Commander.

When it became necessary for men to wear a Divisional sign (early in 1917) the shamrock was adopted. Worked in green silk, in a circle of khaki cloth, it was worn on the arm below the shoulder.

The green diamond-shaped piece of cloth worn on the right arm showed that the wearer had gained one of the Parchment Certificates awarded by the G.O.C. for service under fire.

The Divisional motto adopted was that of the famous Irish Brigade who fought for the King of France, 1690-1790.

17TH (NORTHERN) DIVISION

The "Dot and Dash" of the 17th Division was started by the Divisional Supply Column, which, being Australian, adopted the Morse "A." By a peculiar coincidence, a dot and dash may be said to be the top of the figures "17."

18TH (EASTERN) DIVISION

This sign was introduced by Lieut.-General (then Major-General) Sir Ivor-Maxse, K.C.B., C.V.O., D.S.O., when in command of the Division.

The letters A T N when pronounced rapidly, sound like " Eighteen."

(See also XVIII. Corps.)

19TH (WESTERN) DIVISION

This Division had one of the best known signs in the B.E.F.—the butterfly. The actual designs varied a lot, but the above diagram represents that generally in use— a butterfly of the " Peacock " variety with eyes on its wings.

It has no history, but was adopted before the battle of the Somme, 1916, by Major-General G. M. T. Bridges, C.B., C.M.G., D.S.O., who was then commanding the Division.

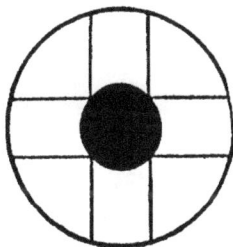

This was quite a simple sign, and appears to have had no particular history. It was a white circular disc, bearing a red cross, which was charged in the centre with a black bull's-eye.

This Divisional sign explains itself,"three sevens" for twenty-one. It is not unlike the six sevens of the 67th Division, and was brought out during the time the Division was commanded by Major-General G. T. Forestier-Walker, C.B., the actual designer being Major-General (then Lieut-Colonel) Clifford Coffin, V.C., D.S.O.

22ND DIVISION

This Division, commanded first by Major-General the Hon. Sir Frederick Gordon, K.C.B., D.S.O., and afterwards by Major-General J. Duncan, C.B., C.M.G., D.S.O., served in France and Salonika. It never used a Divisional sign, but, like the other Divisions in the Salonika Force, had strips of coloured braid worn on the shoulder-straps by the personnel. The distinguishing colour of this Division was black.

(See also 26th, 27th and 28th Divisions.)

23RD DIVISION

This was a most distinctive sign—a Maltese Cross in a circle. The above is a reproduction of one of its stencil signs, which was stencilled in red on a white ground. Its history seems to be at present unknown, for many enquiries have elicited no facts which throw any light on the subject.

24TH DIVISION

There is no particular history attached to the sign of this Division. The design was as shown above, painted in red and white, the black part representing red.

25TH DIVISION

This Division had two signs. The lozenge, or oblong shown above, was painted on the transport vehicles in red and white. (The black portion represents the red.) It has no particular history, being chosen simply as an ornamental marking for the transport.

The real fighting badge of the Division was the red horseshoe "points upwards." When Major-General Sir Guy Bainbridge, K.C.B., took over command of the Division in June, 1916, he arranged for all Regimental Officers and men to wear the horseshoe in red cloth on the back just below the collar. All Staff Officers wore it on the right arm. The horseshoe was a simple design, easy to draw and cut out; the Division had not been very lucky, and it was felt that such a sign would greatly assist esprit-de-corps.

26TH DIVISION

This Division was known by the blue bar worn on the shoulder-straps in exactly the same manner as the buff and green stripes of the 27th and 10th Divisions respectively.

27TH DIVISION

When the Salonika G.H.Q. order came
out that distinctive marks were to be
adopted by all the Divisions in Macedonia,
the 27th Division was given buff for its
particular colour.

This was worn as a narrow strip on each
side of the shoulder-strap, and was painted
on the backs of limbers, gun-carriages, etc.
(in the latter case the colour being about
four inches long and two inches high).

The actual colour used to represent the
official buff ordered varied from the khaki
of a puttee string (very popular and almost
universal among the personnel) to a bright
gamboge supplied by the D.A.D.O.S. for
the vehicles.

28TH DIVISION

This Division, which served in France, and afterwards in Salonika, was distinguished by the narrow red stripe worn on the shoulder-straps by the personnel.

(See also 22nd, 26th and 27th Divisions.)

The peculiar narrow red triangle of this
Division was brought out by the G.O.C.—
Lieut.-General Sir Beauvoir de Lisle, K.C.B.,
D.S.O. It is in reality " half a diamond,"
and was designed to remind all ranks of the
importance of the diamond as a Military
Formation in open fighting, from a Patrol
to an Army.

The General found that junior leaders had
much difficulty in understanding minor
tactics, especially advanced guards, and as
he strongly advocated the efficacy of the
Diamond Formation, he adopted the diamond as the 29th Divisional sign, half
being worn on each shoulder.

The badge of honour, an enamel half-
diamond and wreath, worn on the sleeve
like the green diamond of the 16th Division,
denoted that the wearer had gained a
Parchment Certificate for his gallantry
under fire, and that his name had been
entered in the Divisional Record book.

62

30TH DIVISION

This Division was raised by the Earl of Derby, and distinguished itself on the Somme. The G.O.C.—Major-General Sir John Shea, K.C.M.G., C.B., D.S.O., wanted a sign which would be characteristic of the Division, and obtained the Earl of Derby's permission to use the Derby crest. The exact crest, " an eagle feeding on a child, and standing on a cap of maintenance," was used without any motto and was worked in silver on a black cloth ground.

31ST DIVISION

This Division was composed of Yorkshire and Lancashire men. The badge was two crossed roses with green stalks, on a black circular ground. The left hand one was white, the other red. In the case of Lancastrian Units and the Divisional Artillery the red rose overlapped the white. In the case of Yorkshire Units and other Divisional Troops the white rose overlapped the red.

32ND DIVISION

This Divisional sign was a clever camouflage. "Four eights for thirty-two." The Divisional sign was started by Major-General Sir William Rycroft, K.C.M.G., C.B., and, when he was succeeded by Major-General T. S. Lambert, C.B., C.M.G., the same sign was utilised. Apart from representing "four eights," the sign had no history.

33RD DIVISION

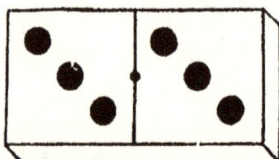

" The double-three Domino."

This was a clever sign, the double three domino for 33 being the explanation. Cards and dominos of various values were very common as signs of various units in the B.E.F., France.

The above sign was very simple, and was selected by the late Major-General E. Ingouville Williams, C.B., D.S.O., who commanded the Division when it arrived in France early in 1916. It originally bore a different badge, but as this was a duplicate of one in use by other troops, the "chequers" came into existence. After the sign was adopted, it was found that if the number 25 (the number of squares in the design) was put down as follows :—

$$
\begin{array}{cc}
1 & 2 \\
1 & 3 \\
\hline
3 & 4
\end{array}
$$

and then added up crossways, the result gave the number of the Division.

This Division had a Bantam Cock as its Divisional sign for a short time, but in 1916-17 a circular emblem of seven fives for 35 was started. This, like the 61st Divisional sign, was a remarkably clever camouflage.

36TH (ULSTER) DIVISION

This is another Divisional sign that needs
no explanation—the " Red Hand of Ulster "
—so familiar as the badge of a Baronet.
The shield was white, the hand red.

37TH DIVISION

"The Golden Horseshoe."

When this Division went overseas in 1915 the number 37 was painted on the carts, etc., but in July, 1916, the G.O.C., Major-General Lord Edward Gleichen, K.C.V.O., C.B., C.M.G., D.S.O., adopted the horseshoe sign. It was the suggestion of one of his Staff Officers, and the points of the horseshoe were shown pointing downwards.

In November, 1916, when Major-General Sir Hugh Bruce Williams, K.C.B., D.S.O., took over the command, the position of the horseshoe was reversed in order " to keep the luck in," and so it remained until the Armistice.

Whenever gold paint could be obtained, the horseshoe was shown in gilt on the wagons, and it was embroidered in gold on the armlets of Divisional and Brigade Staff Officers. It was cut out of chrome yellow cloth and worn on both sleeves by all other officers and men.

38TH (WELSH) DIVISION

The Red Dragon of Wales was a most fitting sign for the Welsh (National) Division. Every officer and man in the Division wore the badge on the sleeve—worked in red on a black square.

The sign meant more to the men, possibly, than the majority of Corps or Divisional signs, probably because it was national and meant something definite, and all were intensely proud of it.

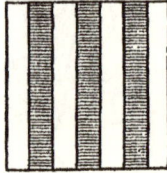

This Divisional sign—a white square with three light (Eton) blue stripes (or, heraldically described, argent, three pallets azure) —was designed by the late General Barnadiston, who took the Division out from England. Its origin is unknown—whether it is heraldic, perhaps a portion of his armorial bearings—or whether it is just a distinctive coloured diagram.

The most careful enquiries have thrown no light on its origin; and, as the designer is dead, it is possible its history will never be known.

40TH DIVISION

When the 40th Division first landed in France in 1915, their Divisional sign was simply a diamond. When Major-General John Ponsonby took over command in 1917 he found out that the diamond was also the sign of another Division. Accordingly a bantam cock was inserted into the sign—the Division having originally been a " Bantam " Division.

When the Division was the first to capture Bourlon Wood, the authorities at G.H.Q. granted permission for the acorn and oak leaves to be added in commemoration of this great feat.

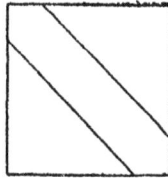

Squares of various colours distinguished
the various formations of this Division, the
distinctive feature being the white diagonal
band which was used right through the
Division. Divisional H.G., R.A.M.C. and
R.E. had the top triangular space yellow
and the lower red ; the Artillery square
was half blue, half red ; the Divisional train
was half blue, half white; and the Pioneers
light blue ; while green marked the 122nd
Infantry Brigade; red, the 123rd; and yellow,
the 124th. As mentioned above, all these
squares had the distinctive white diagonal,
while each Infantry Battalion bore the
number 1, 2, 3, or 4 painted on the Brigade
sign. There was no history attached to the
sign.

42ND (EAST LANCASHIRE) DIVISION

This Territorial Division left England for Egypt in September, 1914. In February, 1915, it helped in repulsing the Turkish attack on the Suez Canal. May, 1915, saw it land in Gallipoli, and early in 1916 it served on the Sinai Peninsular. In March, 1917, it came to the Western Front.

The sign was a diamond, in different colours, with the number of the Battalion, Brigade of Artillery, Field Company, etc., in the centre.

The Divisional colours were red and white—in the above diagram the shaded portion shows the red half of the diamond.

Early in 1918 the G.O.C.—Major-General A. Solly-Flood, C.B., C.M.G., D.S.O.,—adopted the motto " Go one better," believing the spirit it expressed would always carry the Division to success.

43RD, 44TH AND 45TH DIVISIONS

The author has not been able to ascertain if these Divisions had signs. They served in India, and were eventually absorbed into the Indian Divisions. It is very unlikely that they ever had their own devices.

46TH (NORTH MIDLAND) DIVISION

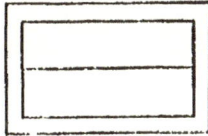

The 46th Division was known by a rectangle of two colours, the top half scarlet; the
lower half green. The rectangle was surrounded by a white border in order to show
it up when it was painted on a dark background. The originator of the sign, Major-
General the Hon. E. J. Stuart Wortley,
C.B., C.M.G., who commanded the Division
at the time signs were instituted, was a
Rifleman, and he incorporated the colours
of the 60th Rifles in the Divisional sign.

47TH (LONDON) DIVISION

This Division was marked by an eight-pointed star. The actual outline of the design was constant through the Division, but the colours of the rim and background varied to distinguish Divisional and Brigade troops.

48TH (SOUTH MIDLAND) DIVISION

The white diamond of the 48th Division has no particular history. When Major-General Sir Robert Fanshawe, K.C.B., D.S.O., joined the Division early in the spring of 1915, he found that the motor cars had this mark, so, later on, when the Divisional sign was started, the white diamond was used.

For some time before this the Supply Column was distinguished by each lorry bearing a portrait of one of Dickens' characters. These were painted by the Interpreter who was attached to the Column.

49TH (WEST RIDING) DIVISION

"The White Rose of Yorkshire."

This Divisional sign was instituted, in the first instance, by Lieut.-Colonel H. V. Kitson, who commanded the Divisional R.A.S.C. He chose the white rose of Yorkshire (in its heraldic form) because the Division was the West Riding Territorial Division, and practically all the officers and other ranks of the Divisional R.A.S.C. were Yorkshiremen. The sign, painted in white, on the tailboards of lorries, etc., enabled those particular vehicles to be easily recognised; and, at night, when driving in convoy, it helped the drivers to see the lorry in front of them. In time, when the Divisional sign was adopted, the same white rose was utilised, and every man in the Division wore a small white rose on his arm.

50TH (NORTHUMBRIAN) DIVISION

When signs were adopted and the 50th Division had to select theirs, the Staff for a long time were unable to select a sign, owing more to the number of their ideas than to the lack of them.

Eventually, however, the suggestion was made that the crest of the G.O.C. (Major General Sir Percival Wilkinson, K.C.M.G., C.B.) should be adopted, and so the unicorn's head, in red, became the Divisional mark.

51ST (HIGHLAND) DIVISION

This sign explains itself, " H D " for Highland Division, but the H is rather carefully camouflaged. Another variation of the sign was sometimes seen in which the H, while attached to the D, was in full block type.

52ND (LOWLAND) DIVISION

This sign, designed by the G.O.C., Major-General John Hill, C.B., D.S.O., explained itself. The ground was white, the " L " for " LOWLAND " black ; the shield was that of St. Andrew, blue, with a white saltire cross, and charged on the cross was the thistle.

53RD (WELSH) DIVISION

This Division served in the East, and all the transport bore the sign of the Prince of Wales' Feathers. Like the dragon of the 38th (another Welsh Division) this was a national sign.

54TH (EAST ANGLIAN) DIVISION

The 54th Division adopted as their sign an umbrella turned inside out. " Umbrella Hill," an elaborately entrenched sand hill about 2,000 yards south of Gaza—one of the strong points of the Turkish defences of Gaza—was raided by the 54th Division in September, 1917, and several prisoners were taken.

Hence the adoption of the umbrella sign.

55TH (WEST LANCASHIRE) DIVISION

" They win or die who wear the rose of Lancaster."

The red rose of Lancaster was the mark of this Division. It will be noticed that it had five petals outside and five inside, while the leaves were arranged five on each side of the stem, thus repeating the number 55.

The rose, embroidered in red silk with green silk stem and leaves on a circular khaki cloth ground, was worn on the arm by officers and men, and was painted on the waggons in a white circular ground, surrounded by a narrow red line.

The G.O.C.—Major-General Sir H. S. Jeudwine, K.C.B.—adopted the rose on account of the Territorial origin of the Division when the latter was reassembled in 1916.

The motto came into use in 1917, and is a quotation from some verses written shortly before his death by the late Captain Watts, who served in the Division and fell in action at Ypres in that year.

56TH (LONDON) DIVISION

" Wat Tyler's Dagger."

This was one of the famous London Territorial Divisions. The Divisional badge was a short sword, the G.O.C.—Major-General Sir Charles Hull, K.C.B.—having selected the sword which forms part of the Armorial Bearings of the City of London.

57TH (WEST LANCASHIRE) DIVISION

This Division was known by the letter " D " on its side. The ground of the sign was black, the straight horizontal bar white, while the remaining curved portion was red.

The Division was raised largely through the efforts of Lord Derby, and the first letter of his name was adopted (turned on its side) as the Divisional Sign.

58th (London) DIVISION

This, originally a second line London
Territorial Division, adopted a castle—
" The Tower of London "—as its sign.
It was sometimes seen with the initials
E H N incorporated in the design, E being
the fifth and H the eighth letters of the
alphabet, while N is the last letter of the
word " Division." The somewhat com-
plicated design shown above was the official
mark, but this was often to be seen in the
modified form of a plain Tower in a circle.

59TH (NORTH MIDLAND) DIVISION

This Division—originally the 2/1st North Midland Division—adopted the Cross of Offa (King of Mercia in 800 A.D.), the Division having been raised in that part of the Midland Counties over which he once reigned. The cross was painted in yellow on all vehicles in the Division, and, cut out of yellow cloth, worn on the back immediately below the collar by all ranks. Divisional and Brigade Staff Officers wore it on blue and red armlets respectively.

This Division first saw active service in Ireland during the Sinn Fein rebellion in 1916. It was commanded by Major-General Sir Nevill Smyth, V.C., K.C.B.

60TH (LONDON) DIVISION

The bee sign of the 60th London Division was very well known. It was brought out by the G.O.C.—Major-General Sir Edward Bulfin—who afterwards commanded the XXI. Corps. At the time he instituted the bee, it was felt that the esprit de corps of the 60th Division had got to be fostered. The indiscriminate drafting of reinforcements up to various units—possibly unavoidable— had destroyed, to some extent, the esprit de corps which existed in formations which had a Territorial designation. It was not by any means an uncommon thing to find men from all parts of England, Scotland and Ireland serving in a particular Division which carried a name implying that it came from a certain part of Great Britain. The Divisional Sign helped enormously in this direction. When Napoleon Buonaparte ascended the French throne, he substituted the golden bee for the fleur-de-lis, which was the sign of the old regime. B stood for Buonaparte. By a peculiar chance it also stood for Bulfin, and the men very quickly knew the allusion the Bee had for their Division.

91

61ST (SOUTH MIDLAND) DIVISION

This was a sign that puzzled a lot of people. It was simply the Roman letters L X I closed up ; very few divined this simple camouflage.

62ND (WEST RIDING) DIVISION

The badge of the 62nd Division was adopted by the G.O.C., who took the Division out to France in 1917—Major-General Sir Walter Braithwaite, K.C.B. (who afterwards commanded the IX. Corps). No particular history is attached to its origin, but the Division used to be known as the PELICANS, and the Yorkshiremen, of whom it was composed, had a saying :—

" When   ta——doock   puts   ta——foot dawn ta——war wull be——well owver ! "

63RD (ROYAL NAVAL) DIVISION

The Anchor sign of the 63rd (Royal Naval) Division needs no explanation. The shape of the cable, flukes of the anchor, etc., varied a little, possibly according to the capabilities of the various artists.

64TH DIVISION

The 64th Division—as far as the author
is aware—never had a sign.

65th (Lowland) DIVISION

This was a Second Line Territorial Division, and never saw service overseas, being disbanded in April, 1918. Its sign was that of the Zodiac for " LEO." The G.O.C.— Major-General G. T. Forestier-Walker, C.B. —adopted this badge because it had not already been appropriated, and also because it would stencil easily. It is possible that, had the Division served overseas, it might have been nicknamed the " Lion " Division, and this would certainly have given some definite interest to the sign.

66TH (EAST LANCASHIRE) DIVISION

The 66th Division sign was a triangle, divided into three bars, the top and bottom being light blue, and the centre one yellow. There was no history attached to the sign, the colours, in three horizontal bands, having been used to mark the Divisional transport. Later, when the Divisional Sign was instituted, the same colours were utilised in triangular form.

67TH (HOME COUNTIES) DIVISION

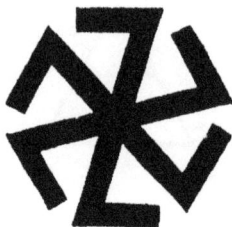

This was a Home Service Division, and was stationed for a long time at Canterbury. There is no history attached to the sign. It was chosen by the G.O.C.—Major-General the Hon. Sir Cecil Bingham, K.C.M.G., C.B., C.V.O.—merely as it described itself.

69TH (EAST ANGLIAN) DIVISION

This was a Home Service Division, and was stationed for some time at Retford. As far as the author can ascertain—and several General Officers were consulted on the matter—the Division never used a sign.

This was a Home Service Division.   Its
sign—to which no particular history appears
to be attached—was a triangle, the top half
being blue, the bottom half red.

74TH (YEOMANRY) DIVISION

The 74th was originally a Yeomanry Division, and was dismounted by the order of the authorities and turned into an Infantry Division. As such, it eventually became one of the finest Divisions we had.

The emblem was a broken spur, selected by the Divisional Commander as a reminder of the sacrifice made by the Yeomen when they gave up their horses.

75TH DIVISION

The 75th Division (commanded by Major-General Sir Philip Palin, K.C.M.G., C.B.) captured Neby Samwil—" The Tomb of Samuel "—a mosque situated on a dominating height four miles from and overlooking Jerusalem. This position was rightly considered the key to Jerusalem, and when it was carried at 11 p.m. on the night of November 21st, 1917, by Outram's Rifles and a Battalion of the D.C.L.I., the Division adopted the key as its Divisional sign.

1st AUSTRALIAN DIVISION

The distinguishing mark of the 1st Australian Division was a rectangle or oblong, with its longer sides on top and bottom, as opposed to the rectangle of the 5th Division, which had its short sides on top and bottom.

Divisional Headquarters had a hollow rectangle, after the fashion of the triangle of Corps Headquarters.

Brigade Headquarters were known by oblongs of plain colours—First Brigade was green, second was red, and Third Brigade light blue.

The Infantry Battalions had two colours arranged as shown on the diagram above. The Battalion colour—either black, purple, brown or white—being on top ; the Brigade colour underneath.

1st AUSTRALIAN DIVISION
(continued)

The colours of the Artillery, red and blue ; Engineers, plain mauve ; A.S.C., dark blue and white ; A.M.C., brown ; were the same in each Division, the patches, of course, being in the Divisional shape.

(See also 2nd Australian Division.)

The Australian Light Horse badge was a rectangle worn in exactly the same position as the above ; but, generally speaking, the colours halved the rectangle diagonally and not horizontally.

2ND AUSTRALIAN DIVISION

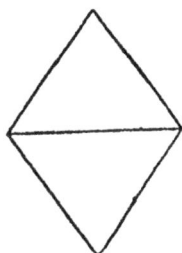

A diamond was the sign of this Division. The system of markings was the same as in the other Australian Divisions. Headquarters had a hollow diamond ; Fifth Brigade, plain green ; Sixth, red ; and Seventh, light blue. The Infantry Battalions had the Brigade colour in the lower half, the Battalion colour in the upper half, the diamond being divided as shown above. The Artillery and A.S.C., on the other hand, had their diamond cut in two vertically.

In addition to the standard colours of the Artillery, A.S.C., etc., mentioned under the First Division, the following colours were also the same throughout the Corps :—

Pioneers—purple, with white edging.
Cyclists—red, with white edging.
A.O.C.—red, with blue edging.
A.A.P.C.—yellow, with blue edging.
Machine gunners—yellow, with black edge and two crossed machine guns in yellow underneath.

3RD AUSTRALIAN DIVISION

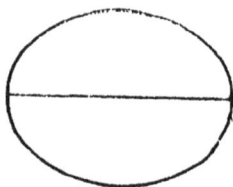

The shape of the sign of the 3rd Australian Division was an oval, as illustrated.

The same system of colouring was in use as described under the headings of First and Second Australian Divisions.

The oval was divided horizontally in the case of the Infantry and Divisional A.S.C., and diagonally in the case of the Divisional Artillery.

4TH AUSTRALIAN DIVISION

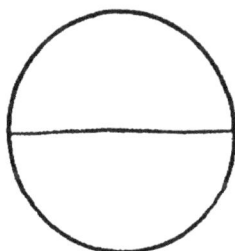

A circle marked the H.Q. of the Fourth Division, and two of the three Infantry Brigades also utilised the circular patch. H.Q., 12th Brigade, had dark blue ; H.Q., 13th Brigade, light blue. The Infantry wore their Battalion colour on top, and the Brigade colour underneath.

Included in this Division towards the end of the war was the Fourth Brigade of the First Division. This Brigade kept its old rectangle, the H.Q. having dark blue, and the Battalions dividing the oblong horizontally, with the Brigade colour underneath.

5TH AUSTRALIAN DIVISION

The Fifth Australian Division had an oblong, but placed in the opposite position to the rectangle of the First Division.

The colours of the Brigades were varied a little, thus :—

8th Brigade had yellow.

14th Brigade had green.

15th Brigade had red.

The Infantry divided their oblong in the manner illustrated, the Brigade colour going on the right, the Battalion colour on the left.

THE CANADIAN DIVISIONS

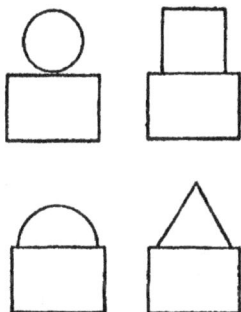

The Canadian signs were very simple, and consisted of the four designs illustrated above, cut out of cloth and worn on the sleeve. The large oblong, about 3″ by 2″, distinguished the Division. The colours were :—1st, red ; 2nd, blue ; 3rd, French grey ; 4th, green. The colour of the second and smaller patch showed the Brigade. Green marked the 1st, 4th, 7th, and 10th ; red the 2nd, 5th, 8th, and 11th ; and blue the 3rd, 6th, 9th, and 12th. The shape of this smaller patch, whether square, triangular, circular, or semi-circular, denoted the Battalion.

Divisional Troops, such as Signal Companies, etc., wore the Divisional patch only. Engineers had the Divisional patch surmounted by the initials " C.E.," while the Machine Gunners were recognised by the Divisional patch surmounted by an arrow, head to the front.

THE NEW ZEALAND DIVISION

The New Zealand Division adopted the national emblem of New Zealand as their Divisional sign. The silver fern—so well known as a chief feature in many of the New Zealand Regimental badges—was placed in a circle, sometimes in white on a black background, and sometimes in green on a white circular ground.

THE RUSSIAN RELIEF FORCE

The Russian Relief Force badge was very well known. It consisted of a white five-pointed star on a background of blue cloth. The shape of the latter, whether triangular, circular, square, etc., varied with the arm of the Force it represented.

PRINTED BY
W HEFFER AND SONS LTD.
CAMBRIDGE, ENGLAND

www.ingramcontent.com/pod-product-compliance
Lightning Source LLC
Chambersburg PA
CBHW030401100426
42812CB00028B/2797/J